Was Body

Poems

BILLIE R. TADROS

Cover art: Rebecca S. Jones
Book design: adam b. bohannon
Book editor: Lisa DeSiro

Published by Indolent Books,
an imprint of Indolent Arts Foundation, Inc.

www.indolentbooks.com
Brooklyn, New York
ISBN: 978-1-945023-25-5

Special thanks
to Epic Sponsor Megan Chinburg
for helping to fund the production of this book.

for Brooke, for what is, and for what remains

CONTENTS

I.

II.

III.

I.

Fun House Mirror Sonnet 1/Invert

Your tongue pulses the well of my body,
a desperate throbbing heart. I pound wanton
for what you look like wearing your organs
outside your pearlbone corset. Ungodly
in slices of Susquehanna Valley
moonlight, all lavender, slick, apparent,
you are easier to touch, ribs unbent
and beckoning like morningsong, and we
can rob each other's cavities this way,
opened and primed for taking, your angry
red meat, my carnal hunger for your blight-
carbon. Your jawbones latched, you try to say
love but it keeps coming out *evolve me*.
Soon we'll find we're rotting from the outside.

Associations with acid:

Tangerine rind and body citric like
critic like sex like loving not the flesh
but its surroundings.

Suggestions of remains stain
like coffee all over the car upholstery
the morning you called and said—

and the fruitflesh bits resurfaced
in the drain long after you'd left.

Associations with opal:

Holes like the ones in your cartilage open
to constellations to fill, as with your earrings—
opaque, pearlescent.

(Think *essence*, think *descent*.)

You are still
so open still
so pierced.

Again-running

In the morning the vessels thick at the periosteum encase (*in case I surround you bones*) your body is a sheath thinning from waking when you're tallest. I remember my father in the kitchen in his underwear his bakery apron folded over the chair. You were a child then in a state with mountains learning the layers. I was decorating cupcakes sometimes in the bakery. This was my histology learning how to write *aorta* over and over again with a pastry bag. You were eating or you were not. It was nervous the sciatica after the eighteen wheeler on the interstate but my father knew only the word for *joints*. You were in Colorado with your hands on either side of the fault lines (*I fault   I fault   I fault*). He had a word for it in his other language but it also meant *tongue*. His tongue had deep fissures. He told me not to jump from the kitchen table like that his tongue had deep fissures from his teeth. He jumped I can see him jumping from the window in that room his brother behind him burning. The scar on his tongue like a sear. Forty years later I was running you were eating or you were not. My father with the scar on his tongue like a sear on the interstate. You were in Colorado with your hands. I was there and I was not dying my patella was wearing. You were thinning he was wearing my favorite shirt. I was running the morning was hot like a sear. We were all alone. He was waiting the pistol sear whose fault. My tongue ached thick as I ran. He weighted the sear the pistol against the scar on his tongue. The mouth the lead encased the vessels thick at the cranial bones. He was tallest in the morning. You were in Colorado or you were not dying. I saw the fault lines in my knee running. Whose fault.

Phantasmagoria: gossamers

Spindling. The whites of eggs
and eyes on the familiar street

and whisked into cocktails.

There were veils
so I thought of you.

Of holding.   Of hiding.

Airfoils, Cross Sections

I.

At a community walk for suicide prevention
the speaker who says *time changes* releases
fifteen doves into the afternoon before ringing
the starting bell.

You understand flight and grip
my open palm like landing.

2.

The first woman I loved crafted coin statuettes—
loose change became steam engines,
skyscrapers, penny nudes held together
with superglue.

I show you my likeness in quarters
with half-wings.

I keep it in an unlocked chest, tell you she left
it for me on the coffee table,

sought lift somewhere else.

3.

That week my sister tries to fly from the rooftop.

Now she sits by the window on the ninth floor
of the behavioral unit of New York-Presbyterian and traces
the flight pattern tattooed over your scapula.

We drink hospital coffee I know you won't keep
down, and when you say I have the same heaviness
you see in her eyes, I know you remember waking
to screaming—I dreamed them
placing the electrodes against my own skull.

(*Trajectories.*)

They pump you with potassium
later that week, send you back
to your life.

We do not talk
about hospitals again.

4.

The first time I am inside
you I take caution, I move
slowly like I am afraid
I might break
you.

The last time I am
inside you I do not know you
will leave, though I map
the jagged scars of entrance
and exit on your dying
wrists.

5.

My ex-lover asks me if I like
the angular way your hollowing
bones in their intersecting trusses
jut from the slight of your back.

I wanted to be that for you, she says,
preens herself for her growing hunger
and gags into my open mouth.

6.

You seek me like fun house mirrors—
convex to your own concave I make
you feel smaller, make you feel
closer. I do not understand
distance.

This is departure:

the distorted image, the leaving
angle.

7.

You draw widows' peaks in pencil
in the margins of your journal, call them gulls,
but I know—

I brushed away the rubber pieces to reveal
my name pinked in shreds over palimpsests
and begged you not to disappear.

Myth of the choleric temperament, or, what gall

Born high-peaked at Laramie
on a llama-gilt morning, she hums
unlike any other hominid,

even the melodies recalcitrant. I crave her
alkaline smile, curved into the most basic
basal cell, she milks me like sugar beet, calls me

her colostrum and lies hippocratic
in the paper hotel about harm. So disarming,
her aviation dreams like propellers.

And, oh, bile beguile, she comes across

such the sophisticate in her champagne
stockings, all the legwork for trickery
tight behind sucked teeth tonic.

Variable:
  x admits light.

Shrimp in their limpid casings.

Her red negligee, hung at the street-
facing window, membranous as lacewing
layer over a wound.

The momentary swell of her starved
body before exhalation, perfectly blown glass.

Olives remind her of whaleskin,
and so the diet is song.

Most fever has reason, and so
there is cause for heat. All of her

logic is heliocentric, I still see
the bulb of her.

Nude with puzzle piece

Look for ground colors
in the corners usually
these are the corner pieces
usually the coroner will look
under her fingernails
for other pieces.

The one she is holding
is blue she was trying
to hold a straight-edged cut
of estuary.

Nude with flowerpot

Terra cotta and earthbone
structure of the sown, the sound
is high this time of year.

She is cracking in all the right places.

(Seeping.)

Sunbaked and ready
for growth they find her
formed to the banks.

(Seedy.)

Myth of the phlegmatic temperament, or, the hack with it

Formed from bare copse bark, she's barely
redolent of the arboreal. I call her Aurora,
though she rarely registers light

and wipe the rime from her surface, notched
like stucco, lacunae like entry, but she's
stolid. I encircle her trunk and she stills, lopping

my love notes with the most composed melodies.
Callused arms, she eaves me there, so I name her ax and puncture
this embrace axis, sapped and coughing catarrh.

Cellar Door: theme and variations

1.

I sell her dolor, jarred.

We are both afraid of botulism.

2.

Seal or adorn: the jar is still just
a jar.

Both frightened and compelled
by containment we draw each other
inside our little glass walls.

3.

Fission: cell ardor. So moved to fuse
we split, fissure.

4.

She paints her cell door green, leaves
it ajar.

5.

She's seldom jarred.

Swelter sores.

6.

Swell.

Terser: sore.

Acreage: theme and variations

1.

The acres' edge, how many furlongs.

Where we were was stretches of corn.

2.

I ached her edge, my tongue along a

longing. What was field. What was feel.

3.

An actor's agile body, everything

you moved inevitable. Furrows.

4.

I asked her. A just question, just

what were we growing to find.

5.

An asterisk: adjust your expectations, fit

them to this squat thrust of star-hungry land.

Phantasmagoria: crocuses

I watch you grind
slate between your
teeth, seeking chalk-

white. Weary echoes,
your enamel wears
thin, acid bearing

saffron, your mouth
an autumn bloom.

II.

Fun House Mirror Sonnet 2/Refract

Like light through a transparent medium
you angle in incident, redirect,
curve and curl inward like fingers in sex
or around the stem of wine crystal, some
sordid circus trick, all bending exits,
all distorted mouths all screaming *entry*,
vacuum invitations, and you want me
but there's no point of—origin, exist—
just ever-arcing and the ricochet
of your body against its fiberglass
walls, flexion, flight contained in chrysalis
form, you are your own entrapment kiss.
Seep me within your hourglass
stall till I shape to your sides, warp and fray.

Postcard Left Unaddressed/1
(Pictured: the upstairs window beneath the broken
curtain rod)

In the backyard, fermented apples, so in the mornings sometimes
I wake up and the neighbor's dog is stumbling just inside the perimeter.

(Fences don't divide, they just outline.)

I collected them all in a paper bag and now it's all rot-
bottomed-out, and I've spent a lot
of time thinking about that night you slept
in your own vomit in the middle of the living room.

It's fall again. There's mulled cider.

I have your sweatshirt when you get cold.

Postcard Left Unaddressed/2
(Pictured: behind the empty fishbowl)

Your mom called last week to ask how I was and if I had heard from you.

I told her, *Seashells*, so I think she thinks you're at the beach

because it was too hard to explain I can hear you dying
if I press my ears against the apartment walls
like they say you can hear the sound of the ocean.

Nude with hailstones

It is barely after the storms the stones
hard bared over her body a child
asks about melting point and indicates
the dark pool between her legs a mother
pulls her child away.

Someone says something sacrificial
about the surrounding yellow tape.

Her hands are held holding.

There is a coil of bungee cord
behind her as though someone
pulled the ice from the sky.

Hollandaise

You pour the sauce into glass
bowls beside the summer colors of your salad

take your routine three bites, touch
your tongue to the fork
tip and nod, it's perfect—

smooth, viscous—find that the stove needs
tending until I have finished

eating, insist

that you have had enough.

You separate the rest of the yellows
and whites and I do not say anything.

I take larger forkfuls, make a spectacle
of my appetite as if this will make you

want.

The flavor is metallic and lemon
sour and smells of consequence—

I am starting to know—

not when you disappear after dinner
but when you clap out your rug, reorganize

your pens (*retract*), when you recoil
at my fingers above your hips (*retract*),

when you try to explain that it's not about
size, that it's not about weight, that you feel

cluttered. This is what it looks like:

the fresh yolk of an egg, bright
yellow and semisolid, the illusion

of containment in cupped hands

but while you're sending it between palms, interlaced
sieve fingers trying to make something out of a center

what's left falls silently between the spaces
and pools on the countertop.

These are remnants.

What I mean to suggest

is that we sift ourselves
to nothing.

Weatherglass Prayer

Have you ever seen trees invert like that, weeping veins.
You are my bloodletting weather, my seeping vain

attempt at drainage while a perennial snowfall.
I tell you *revolver, circumvention,* the cheap winged weathervane

is all circles again. This is unseasonable egress, the cartilage
ground given to torrent along the creeping vein:

I am your fault line viaduct. Wind-rent, you rendered me
winter splay. I am tired of keeping vein

tectonics, so here you quake and liquefy, precipitate avulsion.
Magma blossom, tide rose, I pine in your deep spring vain.

Phantasmagoria: peel peal appeal

You unzip your rubber
suit like butterflied
lobster tails.

I've got callus
peelings and all night
to talk about exoskeletons.

Steamed, they're not screams,
merely the release of air
through the mouthparts.

Phantasmagoria: darkroom

You rip the negatives from the strip
and swallow them with cheap wine.

When they call to tell me you've ruptured
your stomach lining, I think only
of flashes.

g   unning

        morning   vessels thick   *I*
surround   your body   when
        I remember my father
            folded over the chair   You were
                 layers I was
sometimes   histology learning how to
write *aorta* over and over again   You were eating
you were   nervous   sciatica after   eighteen
        but   knew only the word for *joints* You
were   Colorado with   fault lines (*I*
fault   I fault   I fault)   a word for   language
but it also meant *tongue*   deep fissures He told me
not to   like   deep
fissures from his teeth   I can see him
     in that room   burning
     like a sear Forty years later I was   eating
you were not My father with the scar on his tongue like a sear
       You were   Colorado with your hands I was
      my patella   wearing You were
     my favorite   I was running   hot
like a sear   alone He   the pistol   whose
fault My tongue ached   as I ran   the
pistol against   The mouth
       bones He was tallest in the morning You
were   or you were   dying I saw   lines in my
knee   Whose fault

Variable:
   x emits light.

Bell of her wine glass, aptly formed
as the well of her chapped mouth
gasped open, the similar expulsive
shapes of climax and purge.

Her skin and the spaces between
my fingers in want and the floodlit
gas station parking lot, the painted
lines, the cheap coffee, the dream
in which those hands flaked skeletal
like the California pepper tree.

These days I wear dark glasses
because I believe in sanctum.

These days her shirts are perfect bleached.

These days I am tired of bone games.

Fun House Mirror Sonnet 3/Warp

You're twisty and all winding, warm and wet,
and like a cheap pine shelf, I absorb you,
I absolve you of your ruin. Soak through,
I'll pretend it's nutritive. I'll abet
your mode and moat of destruction, pooling
yourself in my center till the bottom
drops out. You are my warbling siren song
breaking mirror glass. Now I'm seeing things.
It's your wily curvature, all gentle
arcs to jagged points, the slope of the knife,
the deadly bend of the highway on-ramp,
off-ramp, your smile in the treacherous lamp
light a false invitation, a love rife
with warning, undertow: distortion pull.

Piecemeal

1.

Sex is expectant.

Run the words together—sex, pectin—as in
that which binds. (The skeleton.)

2.

You two.
You too are—expectant.

I watch you pull on your jeans and cry
and still I have to tell myself when I dress
that this is not my fault.

(I keep seeing ivory, angles.)

3.

       (break: line, time, bone)

You say, *Sorry*, your joints fraying.

4.

You are why I love the notion
of a fossilized hatching,

both the breaking and the frozen
potential for survival preserved.

5.

I take a quiet photograph: the curvature
of your neck, break it with parabolic cuts
into puzzle pieces.

What is done next to the photograph
is what I would like to do to what's left
of your body, piecemeal.

Ride Ticket

A Ferris wheel spelling
appellations, bulb color.

Spinning does it, the way
your circles are.

I tell you I am carnival dreams,
I am carnivorous and you dangle
like dried meat from the top car
groaning metal, salt rises to the skin
of your thin arms, cures.

Self-preservation, your shelf
reservation, you, a shell, a resin.

Skinning does it, makes your circles.

Cycle, recycle your cells, like anagrams
I no longer know your given
name, shriven, I node-linger
in this trellis.

I dwell on platforms waiting
for light essays at night.

Thinning does it, the sway you work in scars.

How does this fireworks show read to you
at your pinnacle, pine tree angel.

The pinning dossier:
stays, sores, spars.

Your poetics of endlessness is bound
by a lever, I pull you pull out and stop.

Because a line has no endpoint

for Kathryn

I.

If I tell you it hurts I presume you'll ask *where*. The spangled bruise on my inner thigh, pointillistic. I'll tell you I threw my fist at it this week to keep it tender—it's my only lasting impression of your lips.

2.

I know how to fire a gun, you say when I indicate the healed points of his contact, now flesh-color cooling. You kiss each gently, and I recall our first night over blueberry table wine, how I told you my father put a pistol in his mouth, how yours taught you to shoot.

How both of these were lessons in survival.

3.

We talk about lines. You draw one from me with two fingers.

Later you put the same two fingers to the back of your throat, cry *empty*.

4.

We make desperate, emptying love in your loft bedroom for the first time in eleven months, both saying, *Still, still*. I take your hand down my side between hip and breast, tell you a tattoo artist in Pittsburgh will render a line there next month.

You always talked about lines.

5.

You fall asleep still drunk, on wine, skin. Water:
You taste like water, you say. *Like need.*

I wake to your spastic intakes of breath, hear the churning in your
stomach. Wonder if you've eaten this week.

I dream of asphyxiation.

In the morning, I ask you if you are hungry.

Thirsty, you say, filling
the well beneath my ribcage.

Parched.

6.

We sit outside the coffee shop parallel to the river, whispering words on each other's palms with our fingertips. Because I am leaving, I think of my father. Because I am leaving, you look at me and say, *Still.* Because I am leaving, your eyes look just like his.

III.

Phantasmagoria: cribbing

Barnyard stalls in ruins, bales
strewn and paint chips wraith

breaths splintered
in the nascent funnel cloud.

You, at the edge of the corral

kicking earth as the landspout
forms, your splintered front
teeth anchored to the post,

your mouth gasped open, recall
the shape of hunger, your neck
tight sinew sucking back the hollow
of your larynx, a supercell.

Associations with erasure:

After her third hospitalization
she was rubbing her thumb against her
forefinger to remove the prints.

My hands, she said,
they want
to forget.

I called you
but you were bent over
my letter with permanent
marker making holes.

Associations with tulle:

We saw that movie about the dancer,
the satin pointe, the final
arabesque.

Teach me about extension
in leaving.

In the movie she is reaching
away, and, yes, you can
elegize the dying with their own
words, I've been wearing yours
as a veil I can't stop
dancing.

Postcard Left Unaddressed/3

   (Pictured: the stoop where you often smoked and
   carelessly tossed your cigarette butts into the
   neighbors' garden)

The street flooded. Imagine the whole building out in the yard
with pots and buckets trying to collect, like we were thirsty. And
plunging for the rose bushes, like we could save the blooms, like
they were holding their breath there under the water just waiting for
our desperate garden-gloved hands.

I want you to know I'm not expecting you to get better
and that I threw out the dried flowers. I couldn't take them anymore
all upside down and hanging in the front closet and smelling
like something I already knew was coming.

Postcard Left Unaddressed/4
(Pictured: the vanity table missing its mirror)

I've been spending a lot of time at the gym since you left.
I've never really been much for numbers or for that macho
pissing-contest how-much-can-you-bench bullshit, but
I realized the other day that I could lift the whole of your body
and press it.

So this is just to tell you that I cried openly
and took the scale out of the women's locker room
and threw it in the dumpster outside.

Nude dis(as)sembling a fire escape

The skeleton is just framework
or what-remains you can hide
you can can it there is a very
large receptacle at the bottom
of the ladder.

She was trying to break
a way to break away.

Nude with circular saw

She wanted to circumscribe be
circumscribed it's circumstantial
that letter he left in the hole he left
in her body that said he just wanted
her to open up he wanted to open her
wanted to fill her with water the river
flooded that afternoon.

It turns out the body
is hemispherical and responds
well to division.

Myth of the melancholic temperament, or, the anti-body

It looked like foie gras
but went down ferric.

I thought I was being ironic when I said
maybe her cooking was rusty,

but for the next three courses she cried
caul-like, fetal, pleading *lean*.

Her splenic lean-to was sloped like arctic
slumber, so I called her igloo.

Peremptory with her freezing points, she was
icicle-tongued and sharpstuck

rooftop drippings, but puddled red
pulp at my touch.

Reactor

For the anniversary of the breaking we built a fall-out shelter in the
    backyard—
concrete, lead, dry earth packed from the garden section of the hard-
    ware store.

We cut down the trees (radiation rains from branches) and left

our clothes outside the blast hatch to minimize the *hot* introduced,
    rubbed
our bodies together below ground: a new shape for memory. We
    planted

a single mustard plant in a patch of earth under the heat lamp, nurtured

it like anxiety, always just a little more water than it
thirsted, slowly depleting our steel thermos provisions.

What happened was more like an earthquake was more like a
    shaking

up, but you grew up just outside Three Mile Island where they said
    they tasted metal
when the nuclear reactor malfunctioned, so you shivered when you
    saw the plumes

feathering from the donut factory on our drive out of town for
    morning coffee

before our burial, a living time capsule:
This is what we did to feel safe.

Dendrochronology

A bullet lodged
in the trunk of a sapling.

Bark blooms
shoots around it.

A child sticks his finger in the open mouth
of a hose the water rushes
radiates
         circlebursts.

You are the finger I am
the water.

Or you are the bullet.

Either way, outripples,
growth rings.

Voicemail on Your Birthday
Three Years after You Didn't Do It

Because it's morning now in that backyard and the river is
cresting and soon the floodwaters will be at the door of the café,

I'm calling to tell you happy birthday and I'm sorry
your eyes were always gravity and I never knew where

to put my hands.

That's why I looked at you with that green immediacy
when you sleepwalked your way into your car

and drove to the grocery store.

When you came you writhed with seizure, so that winter was ecstatic
danger, like how you would stick your fingers inside me

then hold them like triggers against your skull, mouth
goodbye over and over in sleep.

Fun House Mirror Sonnet 4/Fray

Think of horsehair, a violin bow rent
and scraping a melody: this is how
you call to me, asking for shreds, and now,
forked I spread myself, your fissure event,
your diverging, your halved understanding
of song, splintered. Think evergreen needles
parted to hang your tokens, and, seedless,
the remnants weeping to the floor, meaning
everything you plant splits like wood, the ax
of your lustmetal driving trunk ripples
until I can't count, quantify the rot,
or seek bloom. This is everything you're not
as the wholeness of forests. This love fells
a plundered harvest. You, love, sap the wax.

Phantasmagoria: lush

Breathwritten words on fogged
glass spell your pretext, mirror

the heart you drew on the hood
of my car, your thinning fingertips
dipped to the third joint

in thick pollen, my joints gummed
with dried beer, honey,

the residue of your body.

un

                vessels
surround   your body   when
           I remember
                            You were
                    layers   I was
                                 learning how to
write *aorta* over   You
you were   nervous   sciatica
                                    You
were   Colorado with   fault
               I
        meant *tongue*   deep
                    I can see
      that room   burning
      like a sear   Forty years later
    you were not   like a sear
        You were   hands
                        You were
                              hot
like   the pistol   whose
fault   ached
                      mouth
           bones   You
were   dying   lines   my
        fault

Variable:
   x remits light.

The pitcher of house ale she ordered for us
to share and the suburban medium
who claimed to know my father.

Definitions of *commune*.

Metallurgy, or the sharp new taste of her
clitoris after the Pine Street tattoo parlor.

The erectile implies blood, which implies both
reflection and absorption, and certain frequencies.

She has absolved herself of me
but I was there and the light on her
back and the light on her back.

Lighter fluid: theme and variations

1.

Light or flutes, her cylinders.

What illumines a votive.

2.

Lied, or fluent, as she told

me about half-life, burn time.

3.

Lye tour flumes, we channel

we try we tie we cleanse.

4.

Like airfoils cutting air

there's fireflight curved.

5.

Like her falls I've lost

what is ignition.

Warfare: theme and variations

1.

Wares for—munitions, store.

Real violence is in preparation.

2.

Worse for a broken shelter,

the ruined well a thrombosis.

3.

Warfarin—after the swallow

I begged her to stop bleeding.

4.

Wherefore I tell you now because

of all the collapsed causeways letting.

5.

Wear four pockets like cardiac

chambers, vacant maps.

6.

We're foreign now as clotting

factors we learn to close.

Myth of the sanguine temperament, or, she's so vein

We built an interisland highway for the sake of arrivals after
her archipelago gesture cleaving. It was steep

upward gradient and mirrored an emaciated landfall, pave-set
onto the alluvial banks and stretched arterial across the river

mouth. When you have measured the distance from the surface
of your skin to your carotid, you can call this capillary, vagus.

Her vaguest unquestionable music, she played the mouth organ
longing on basalt beaches, waiting for docking. It's important

to know about geography and sediment, the forests
of inhabitable trunks there host to blight and gravity, and this

was her garden with all of the car-shaped holes
I drove circles through. Excuse my circumlocution. I was nervous,

it was a system. She was liver, I was lover, this was body.

Epithalamion

for Kathryn

I.

epithet:

You wore a veil
and heavy matte

the train was bound
for Penn Station   I was bound

      to you   I was bound to   do this

      our painted
faces   facing both

      ways like rails   like

history   locked   wrists mock   cuffs

You kissed me so hungrily   years later

there are still   red pangs

(and the echo of a house   with columns

  a local paper that captioned   how

you wanted to marry me   *To be able to*)

Don't apologize for your new   stills your wine

your truffles   the Arno River

    or your ring—   to be able to—

    I'm building a wall:

dike   dyke   it's all

collapsed it's all   the same

2.
epithalamus:

I was inevitable   or the body

                    that embodied your inevitability

Not like a conveyor belt   you say

                    Like a current

This is connection   survival

                    marriage   pinpoints

the pineal gland

                    and all of your darkness   what

hope of regulation

You're circling your circadian

rhythms rigor

                    mortis   how I can't

unclench this

fist this   net
work your   ulterior   arterial

        knot

His proposal limns the limbic

Nothing you or I can control

3.
epithymy:

A whole is just parts that refuse

to acknowledge their loneliness

the way you come   archaic

      to the touch

a pit   like mine I couldn't

mine you   mind you   your

      cartouche   inscribed

when you told me you had pierced

      your clitoral   hood   I kept

racing like blood

        flow to you   your sores   your

source   you're sorting

      the vessels   I buried

4.
epithem:

Rapt like gauze in your bride   white

      flax   you closed

the door and opened
       and I haven't found another

way to say what you felt   like   soothe

smooth against

               my palm

      a prayer
            a salve

5.
epithelium:

You're avascular   packed   and selective

absorption
            I sin for you   I skin for you

but the song is nervous tissue now

You're innervated   I'm enervated   you're

            stratified and I'm not

your cell anymore

You mention something about currents
again   about surfacing
                                    but I'm back

in that studio on Pine

where you told me I tasted   held

against the soft

            palate   like water

6.
epitheca:

Enclose ensheath   the theca fully

      how you take him

      how you took my hand inside

your mouth   the mouthfeel

      how I felt to you   how I felt you

    empty yourself

No longer what you know of consumption

      I run   my body   clean

This is the gutting   how you lay

exhausted   on the kitchen floor   your chest

    heaving   the gentle cave

      forgetting   the hole

Postcard Left Unaddressed/5
(Pictured: a shallow depression in the linens, your
side of the bed)

I went to dinner with a new woman last night.
     Her body was like driving in a new city, a foreign grid.

When I made love to you I often thought of coloring books,
of the dark

     outlines of images, the shaded chambers of your ribs.

From my window I watch the switchboard lights
     alternate and disappear, delicate circuitry, and you

wrap yourself in your old college sweatshirt against the night
of another

     weather grieving a quiet
     meteorology, like waiting for rain

and ask how high the water is this time of year, where we were.

ACKNOWLEDGMENTS

Grateful acknowledgment is made to the editors of the journals and anthologies in which some of these poems first appeared, sometimes in earlier versions.

Barely South Review: "Airfoils, Cross Sections"; "Dendrochronology"
Bearers of Distance (Eastern Point Press, 2013): "Again-running"; "gunning"; "un"
The Boiler: "Lighter fluid: theme and variations"; "Warfare: theme and variations"
The Collapsar: "Phantasmagoria: gossamers"; "Phantasmagoria: crocuses"; "Phantasmagoria: peel peal appeal"; "Phantasmagoria: darkroom"
Crab Fat Magazine: "Hollandaise"; "Postcard Left Unaddressed/1"; "Postcard Left Unaddressed/2"; "Postcard Left Unaddressed/3"; "Postcard Left Unaddressed/4"; "Postcard Left Unaddressed/5"
Eureka Literary Magazine: "Cellar Door: theme and variations"
Gigantic Sequins: "Acreage: theme and variations"
Glass: A Journal of Poetry: "Associations with acid"
Horse Less Review: "Variable: x admits light."; "Variable: x emits light."; "Variable: x remits light."
Menacing Hedge: "Fun House Mirror Sonnet 1/Invert"; "Fun House Mirror Sonnet 2/Refract"; "Fun House Mirror Sonnet 3/Warp"; "Fun House Mirror Sonnet 4/Fray"
Tupelo Quarterly: "Piecemeal"
White Stag Journal: "Because a line has no endpoint"; "Epithalamion"; "Voicemail on Your Birthday Three Years after You Didn't Do It"

Women Write Resistance: Poets Resist Gender Violence (Hyacinth Girl
   Press, 2013): "Nude with circular saw"; "Nude with puzzle piece"
Yalobusha Review: "Reactor"

Thank you to the readers and mentors at Sarah Lawrence College
who saw the earliest versions of these poems—thank you especially
to Cathy Park Hong.
   Thank you to Sam for seeing, and seeking, the potential in this
manuscript, and to Lisa for helping me to realize it.
   And finally, thank you to the women with whom I shared a
river—and the formative moments that preceded this mythology.

ABOUT THE AUTHOR

Billie R. Tadros is an Assistant Professor in the Department of English and Theatre and an affiliated faculty member in the Women's and Gender Studies Program at The University of Scranton. She is the author of two other books of poems, *The Tree We Planted and Buried You In* (Otis Books, 2018) and *Graft Fixation* (Gold Wake Press, 2021). You can find more of her and her work at www.BillieRTadros.com.

ABOUT INDOLENT BOOKS

Founded in 2015, Indolent Books is a nonprofit poetry press based in Brooklyn, with staff working remotely around the country. In our books and on our website, Indolent publishes innovative, provocative, and risky work by poets and writers who are queer, trans, nonbinary (or gender nonconforming), intersex, women (of all races and ethnicities), people of color (of all genders), people living with HIV, people with histories of addiction, abuse, and other traumatic experiences, and other poets and writers who are underrepresented or marginalized, or whose work has particular relevance to issues of racial, social, economic, and environmental justice. We also focus on poets over 50 without a first book. Indolent is committed to an inclusive workplace. Indolent Books is an imprint of Indolent Arts, a 501(c)(3) charity.

CPSIA information can be obtained
at www.ICGtesting.com
Printed in the USA
LVHW110120221222
735707LV00004B/708